AF429972

I PROMISE TO LOVE ME A LITTLE MORE

I PROMISE TO LOVE ME
A LITTLE MORE

I PROMISE TO LOVE ME A LITTLE MORE

I PROMISE TO LOVE ME A LITTLE MORE

N. NICKOLA FREEMAN

Contents

DEDICATION

I want to dedicate this book to my sister, Venessa Freeman.

She has inspired me to grow, know, and love myself a little more.

This book is also dedicated to all individuals who want to intentionally love themselves more and be comfortable and at peace from within.

ACKNOWLEDGMENTS

I sincerely appreciate those who supported my journey as a self-published author. The discipline of writing and publishing took many unforeseen turns, but your buttress remained steadfast. I am fortunate to have this kind of association.

Narda, who finished this book's cover, and to the many people who voted in the selection of the cover.

I also want to thank the individuals who provided insights into this book's layout and polished appearance.

Most importantly, I want to acknowledge Jehovah for adding another dimension of purpose to my life by giving me inspired thoughts and the fortitude to put this book together for those who will read and benefit from its contents.

Before you start reading:

Say a prayer that your eyes and heart may be opened to ways to know you better and grow in your love.

Engage your forward-looking mindset and prepare to take time to uncover your answers to some of the questions asked.

Smile.

Now, let's go...

Introduction

For far too long, we've listened to others and bought into their thoughts about ourselves; often, these thoughts were not a good story or a positive picture.

Make it your life's purpose to think assuredly about you, your personality, your talents and what you have to offer this world. Certainly, this world would be different without you (You should own this last sentence).

I hope this book stirs the hearts and minds of many who are looking for constructive change within themselves. I intend to challenge my readers to think beyond the improbable notion that it may not be possible to love themselves without being selfish or self-centered. And not to believe it is trivial to love oneself on a deeper and more practical level.

There are no two ways to do it; the work will be challenging, but it is certainly worth an attempt - even several attempts. Amid the difficulties you may face on this path, never give up on yourself, not now, not even later.

"Love your neighbor as yourself" is a command that was issued. Over the years, this command has been repeated in the everyday setting without much thought or practice behind the deeper meaning of such a significant and well-needed command. Although this phrase has been popular in many communities, I have never heard anyone ask these questions. What if you don't love yourself? How can you then love your neighbor? Is this command not a plethora of unconditional love that should be showered on your neighbor? Isn't the essence of this command, therefore, a commission to erase the ignorance of not knowing how but to go and learn how to love yourself unconditionally so that you may be able to love your neighbor? While these questions aim to position you to love your neighbor, let's pause at knowing how to love yourself unconditionally for a minute. Doing some house cleaning before going outside to do some work is imperative.

The intent of unconditional love must come from a reservoir where love resides. Is it not easier to love someone when they are in your good graces? That's conditional love. How often are you in good grace with yourself?
The depths of love or love for yourself cannot be uncovered within these pages, but this is a good place to start, and/or to expound your reservoir of love. We will never exhaust the cenote of love in this lifetime; we should, however, try to exhaust each other with unconditional love.

Matthew 22: 36-39 (KJV)

"Master, which is the great commandment in the law? Thou shalt love the Lord thy God with all thy heart, and with all thy soul, and with all thy mind. This is the first and great commandment. And the second is like unto it, thou shalt love thy neighbor as thyself"

Don't Forget About Yourself

I don't think you hate yourself, but I don't think you love yourself unconditionally either. No one is as hard on you as you are on yourself. How can you love yourself a little more? The concept of love may get lost when the beam is shone on you as an individual because the common notion says if you love yourself, you are selfish or have become self-centered. This notion has been proven to leave people in the sun without nutrients or nourishment for their souls; therefore, they have become bitter, angry, and unhappy. These would be the essentials left to formulate the tentacles of your personality and how you relate to others. Many people who possess these discourteous traits are like empty shells, perhaps with a delightful smile.

Often, we forget about ourselves. Our focus is centered on others - the kids, spouse, boss, friends, parents, and neighbors - and what they require of us. Stop; the beam is now on you. Let's get down to the naked you by minusing others and the fluff. That would be the elegant clothes, shoes, cars, jobs, jewellery, and make-up - all tangible items.
What's left?
Essentially this is a scary thought for some, but it will be the most attractive thing to get to know yourself a little better.

Knowing You on a Deeper Level

Take a deep dive into the thoughts behind some of your actions. Why do you make certain decisions? Do your decisions follow a certain pattern? What emotions are triggered just before those decisions are made? Did those emotions derive from a place of familiarity? Are these past emotions influencing your present decisions? When did you decide to become less flexible with these types of decisions?

Take all the time you need to uncover your answers.

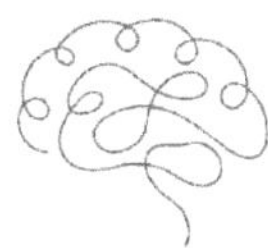

This concept opens the door to knowing you on a deeper and

more honest level.

After a situation has played out, ask yourself why you chose to react the way you did or made a particular choice. Then try to trace such a tendency to the first time you had a similar encounter. Tracing or revisiting the past oftentimes leads to a painful place. This is the time you will need to permit yourself to be vulnerable to you. At this point, you must be gentle with yourself and develop the trust that you are willing and capable of caring for yourself during these aching moments.

Tell your heart that you want to hear what it has to say about each painful experience. Then listen.

Allow your heart to open to you. Do not smother, dismiss, or shut down what it has to say.

What needs did you have that were unmet at that time? Prepare to accept that part of you with unmet needs such as rejection, not being valued, abandoned, forced, disliked, disrespected...

Validate your pain. For example, you can say to yourself, I know that was a painful experience and I'm sorry you had to go through that.

Recognize what emotions accompany those painful experiences and what definite statements or promises you made. Most times it starts with, "I Will Never".

This exercise will help you realize your triggers and what feeds your behaviors. It is a powerful tool for making changes or concretizing favorable behaviors.

Deserving Your 'Own' Love

We all want to be loved but look for that from others instead of giving it to ourselves first. Have you repeatedly put others before you no matter how painful it was?
Why?

Could it be, you don't want to seem selfish?
OR
Could it be you don't think you are deserving of your 'own' love?

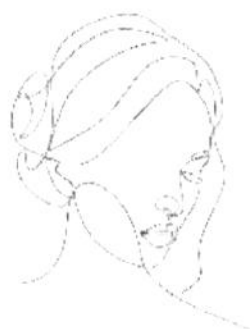

When is love deserving?

A better question is, when is unconditional love deserved? Are you willing to remove the conditions surrounding your love so that you may benefit from it?

You probably were taught to put others first so that they may arrive and dwell in the space of 'happiness' created by you. If you put others before yourself at the expense of being in pain, you will be the last to arrive at the 'happy' environment that you created. The challenge to putting others first at the expense of your being in pain is that this would be a façade.

Stop creating moments of façade and be intentional about creating authentic moments. Please do not take this as a blanket statement that you should never make sacrifices for people. But constant self-neglect will never benefit you or anyone.

How about we all arrive at the event of joy together?

Take the time to know yourself, what makes you joyful, and what purpose you should fulfil in the days you are afforded. The idea of being left behind is archaic. If each person operates from a place of wholeness, no one will be left behind in pain or darkness. This would eradicate the fearful thought of losing yourself, which occurs more often than is admitted.

Self-Sabotage is Self-Imprisonment

What unfavorable decisions keep you kicking yourself and committing the act of self-sabotage repeatedly?

When you constantly kick yourself over one or more situations, you are preventing growth. You inadvertently remain in the same place, not learning from your mistakes. When does the kicking stop?

If you self-sabotage, how do you expect to grow and reach

your full potential for your family, job, school, finances, friends, and religious life?

Did you know that if you sabotage yourself, you permit others to do the same to you?

Self-sabotage is another word for self-imprisonment. In the mental field, you hold yourself captive and apply punishment that you deem necessary for the crime that was committed. This would be equivalent to putting yourself in a corner of your home for making a mistake on the first day of work. For the next few weeks leading to months and still going, each day when you return home from work, you see yourself sitting in that corner, and you repeat how stupid you are for making that silly mistake. You shrink more in that corner each day. The worst part is that you find other negative adjectives to pile on the others that were already dished out. Now you are angry, mortified, humiliated or anxious and you don't feed yourself. You shrink even further in your corner. Your shrunken spirit exudes from your being and bursts through your smile. Bullies are like a hound to the scent of blood; they rush to the kill. Here come the bullies to your shrunken, dying spirit. Usually, the punishment does not fit the crime and the sentencing for the crime doesn't have an end date.

When you recognize your mistakes, comb through the event/s for lessons and become proficient at not repeating the blunder/s. This will give you the freedom to operate as an individual without the shackles of your negative verbiage.

Dark Secrets are Malignant

What dark secrets do you hold, regardless of how

much they eat away at your soul? Darkness and secrets are malignant and burdensome, yet one carries them around for years. The weight of such malignancies slowly but gradually will cause the death of your spirit. Anything that slowly deforms you must be dealt with with great urgency. There is nothing hopeful to gain from these gnawing varmints.

Over time you may think you have forgotten about your

darkness because it is no longer a part of your everyday life. This is where your heart and body compensate or cover up for you. Seemingly, this is a beguiling thing, but this is called underlined stress. Stress is a catalyst for many diseases that plague the body.

Do not hold on to stress like you cannot exist without it. Free yourself from the cuffs that bind you to these malignancies. If you have dark secrets hidden in the recesses of your heart for years, the easiest thing to do is to carry on as though you are okay. It is not okay to intentionally keep yourself in an unhealthy state. Reaching a healthy place may take work, but it would be worth the effort.

Some burdens and secrets require the help of a trustworthy person, such as a counselor, a pastor, a therapist, or a professional psychologist.

One source of help that many forget or may neglect because of the view placed on Him - seeing Him as one sees their earthy parent/s – the person who sternly disciplines or the one who doesn't care about the 'simple things' that they are concerned about. Elohim Ahavah, the God who loves simply because He loves, will come to your rescue in a heartbeat. Just ask Him to. Philippians 4: 6-7 says, "Be careful for nothing; but in everything by prayer and supplication with thanksgiving let your requests be made known unto God. And the peace of God, which passeth all understanding, shall keep your hearts and minds through our Lord"

There is always a way for the one who desires to be healthy in mind, body and spirit.

Limiting Pain's Time with You

Are the memories of painful events taking priority seating in your mind?

It's a memory, which means it is in the past. Learn the five stages of grief:

Denial
Anger
Bargaining
Depression
Acceptance

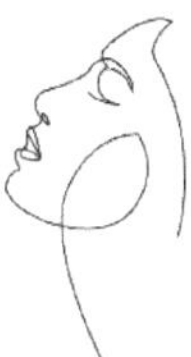

The first two stages are the most difficult to move away from

because, on the surface, they justify the painful event.

Persons unknowingly stay within these phases for years. Aim always to reach the fifth stage. Here, you will have peace.

While experiencing pain is inevitable, people tend to make this a fixture in their lives. This is never meant to be so. Don't hold on to pain for too long, it can become addictive to the point where you live the life of being a victim. As stated before, validate your pain, and take care of yourself while you are experiencing an unfavorable incident but endeavor to move forward.

You can seek to set time limits on the different levels of painful involvements. For example, if someone says something that hurts your feelings, try to speak with that individual in real time, resolve it and then let it go. If you missed an opportunity that you wanted for the longest time, give yourself two to three days to be remorseful then move on. If you experience the end of a relationship, give yourself a few weeks to resolve your pain and then move forward with your life. If you have experienced the loss of a loved one, maybe seek the help of a professional to help manoeuvre through the pain that comes with this.

The essence is never to stay or feel stuck in pain. The healthy way to deal with pain is by accepting its reality in your life but limiting the time it gets to spend with you.

Extend Grace & Mercy to Yourself

It is time to throw down the gauntlet to forgiveness.

Forgive yourself. You deserve it!
Forgiveness means allowing yourself to stop hurting and reframing your painful and negative thoughts into positive ones.
You can do it! Extend grace and mercy to yourself.

Have you ever thought of forgiving yourself?

Should this be a virtue to be extended to only others? If yes, why?

If at any point you can identify that you have done something wrong, you should go a step further after recognizing the wrong and extend forgiveness to the wrongdoer, you.

It's time to stop leaving yourself behind.

James 3: 2 (NIV)

"We all stumble in many ways..."

Proverbs 11: 17 (KJV)

"The merciful man does good for his own soul..."

Your Love Note

Here's a suggestion, write a love note, that will provide healing to yourself.
I will share one that I wrote to myself some time ago:

*Hey there, you look lovely today. It's been a long
time coming but I didn't have the courage,
I didn't have the faith,
And I didn't have the words.
I am now here, looking at you, seeing you and knowing you.
I have caused much hurt, much pain and much anger.
I have turned your mind and left you cold.
I have belittled you in so many ways I can't even start.
I have limited you; I have cheapened your existence.
I have dished out things that had no place with you.*

*I have buried in you dark secrets, things that no one should
have. I know you did a good job keeping them even
to the point where they became yours, and I know you
defended them with your life.
I know you opened yourself to the walls of your home,
and they and no other knew you.
You don't care for me as you should and I
can understand why, Though I wouldn't deny
that you tried.*

*I have taken your talent, but I know you'll find another.
That's one great thing I love about you:
You create options for yourself.
There's more, as it has been a lifetime already.
These are worth mentioning because of the
effect they have on you.
I Am Truly Sorry.*

*I bought you a bouquet of roses and this is
the meaning of it.
The red ones symbolize my truest feelings.
I love you.*

*I apologize, I'm terribly sorry for the pain and hurt I caused.
The white petals represent my apology.*

*The green leaves represent your life and how you should
flourish.*

*The white shrubs are added to accentuate the softness and the
color of the roses – just as you soften and accentuate your
surroundings.*

*Though this bouquet of roses may fade in color
and life as the days go by.
The real reason, the true essence of its meaning and
the reason why I give this bouquet to you will never die.*

*I wish I could take back
The spoken words
The horrific thoughts
The mortified situations
The piercing pains
And the sickness of anger.
But they are already out there for
years now.
I am so sorry.*

*I am happy to have you, me.
I only ask that you forgive me and
love me.
Love me more.*

*I know you have a lot to give and
to be happy for.
I wish the very best for you.
With a kiss and some roses, I give in exchange
for your forgiveness.*

Don't Get it Twisted

You have come this far in knowing how to love yourself as a valued individual. The best part is that there is so much more to gain when you choose to be the person that you love and care for. Don't get it twisted; self-love is different from loving yourself.

Love is never selfish until it becomes self-centered or tainted. Self-love is self-centered, and tainted love is not love.

Loving yourself extends the same measure of kindness to yourself that you would bestow on others in any given situation, favorable or unfavorable.

I wish for you to continue this journey so here are some additional steps to take to love yourself a little more:

Colossians 3: 12 (NIV)

"Therefore, as God's chosen people, holy and dearly loved, clothe yourselves with compassion, kindness, humility, gentleness and patience"

Resentful Mind

Never allow your mind to become resentful.

To reach a place of resentment means expressing indignation or bitterness toward an individual or circumstance. Focus on what you can control and let go of what you cannot. Speak to each situation calmly and ask for what you want so that you can make decisive decisions going forward. Self-control is a crucial component in forming good character traits.

Push yourself above the negative emotions of reacting, but

now respond. To respond is timely, and to react is rash. Therefore, your responses should be timely; there's no rush. In so doing, be very keen that your choice words and actions are confident, uplifting, carefully thought of, and never bitter.

Romans 12: 2 (NKJV)

"...But be transformed by the renewing of your mind, that you may prove what is that good and acceptable and perfect will of God"

Ephesians 4: 31-32 (NLT)

"Get rid of all bitterness, rage, anger, harsh words, and slander, as well as all types of evil behavior. Instead, be kind to each other, tenderhearted, forgiving one another, just as God through Christ has forgiven you"

Stop & Catch Your Breath

Be intransigent about this point; let your world stand still.

Time seems to be running away, and you are running even faster to keep up with it but stop for a while and catch your breath. Spend some alone time realigning your body with what inspires you.

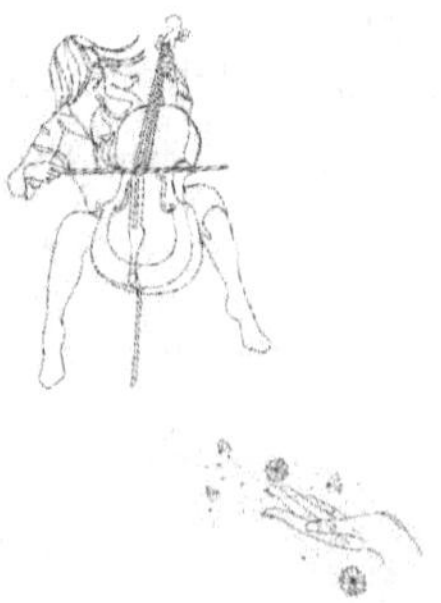

Take yourself on inspirational dates and breathe life into

being you. When you are inspired, endorphins are released, and you become energized again - energized to run alongside time and accomplish more. Did you know that inspiration is contagious?

Psalm 36: 9 (NKJV)

"For with You is the fountain of life; In Your
light we see light"

Exodus 20: 9-10 (NKJV)

"Six days you shall labor and do all your work, but
the seventh day *is* the Sabbath of the Lord your God. *In it* you
shall do no work..."
(He wants you to rest)

Sun-Kiss Moment

Foster your innate senses to become intuitive to the moments your mood **begins** to change negatively. Life happens all day every day, but the crucial point is managing yourself and your reactions. Being this intuitive to the times your mood begins to change doesn't happen overnight. Connect the dots to activities throughout your days; how did you feel when you walked out of your car last evening, and what evoked that? What emotions did you have when you first got out of bed, and why? When you walked into the store, what were your thoughts and how did you feel about them? Know what you are feeling, when and why.

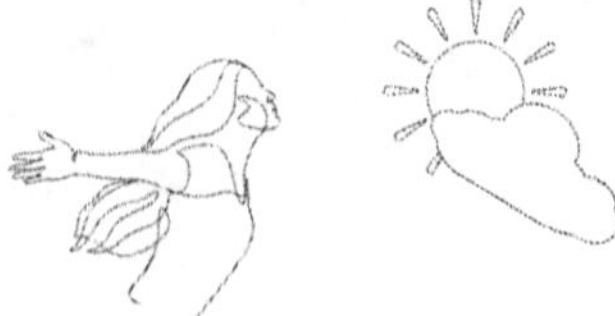

When your gloomy mood arises, now is the time to have a

sun-kiss moment. Willfully choose a random happy thought and seal that in with a long kiss from the sun. Spending a few minutes in the sun increases your vitamin D level and elevates your mood. This will keep you mindful and present in the moment.

Proverbs 23: 7 (NKJV)

"For as he thinks in his heart, so is he."

Compliments

Compliment someone. Their responses are usually pleasant and come with a smile. There are many things that are contagious, and a smile is one of them. Their smile will emit your smile and aid in the relaxation of your mind.

Compliments provide physical and emotional benefits to the person who gives them.

They help to improve physical health by reducing pessimistic emotions. They also aid in muscle relaxation, which will provide a more youthful look. Compliments boost self-esteem, increase resilience to stress, and enhance self-morale and productivity.

An easy way to gain all these benefits, right? You should, therefore, also compliment yourself, DAILY.

I would like to remind you that there is **always** something to compliment someone on.

Proverbs 16: 24 (NKJV)

"Pleasant words are like a honeycomb, Sweetness
to the soul and health to the bones"

Proverbs 27: 2 (NLT)

"Let someone else praise you, not your own mouth—
a stranger, not your own lips"
(You should look to compliment others while others
look to compliment you)

Motivating Footprints

Pour meaningful, fun-loving words into the love tanks of those around you. Too often, people who are not in our immediate circle meet the crass and austere end of our personalities. Choose to make a change, starting with you.

Motivate...
Motivate...
Motivate...
This will add to your sense of purpose in life.

One of the biggest things would be leaving a significant and foundational footprint from the impact you made in the life of a stranger for years to come.

Proverbs 25: 11 (NKJV)

"A word fitly spoken is like apples of gold in
settings of silver"

Ephesians 4: 29 (NIV)

"Do not let any unwholesome talk come out of your
mouths, but only what is helpful for building others
up according to their needs, that it may benefit those who
listen"

You Are 'A' Masterpiece

Speak kind words to yourself daily. Typically, when you look in the mirror, you look for what's wrong and what can be fixed. Let's change this habit to a new one: each time you look in the mirror, identify what's perfect and comely, and speak to it/them with compassion.

You can also use this mirror activity to speak to other bad habits that you want to change.

Words can be limiting, and they can bring about a negative or positive atmosphere.

Choose the latter.
Today, choose to see yourself as a masterpiece, what's right and what's perfect about you.

Proverbs 18: 21 (NKJV)

"Death and life are in the power of the tongue…"

Song of Solomon 4: 7 (NIV)

"You are altogether beautiful, my darling,
there is no flaw in you".

Ephesians 2: 10 (NLT)

"For we are God's masterpiece. He has created us anew…"

Empathize with Yourself

Because pain is such an integral part of life that is often not dealt with healthily, I feel the need to remind you to allow yourself to feel pain, to grieve, be sad and go through moments of disappointment.
Then, move on.

Empathize with yourself. You are human. Life comes with many painful and grievous paths, but try to focus on coping strategies and never judge yourself. Understand that you are responsible for the length of time you spend agonizing. Open your heart to others and let them comfort you. Every day is a new chance to live your life with sweetness.

Ecclesiastes 3: 1 & 4 (KJV)

"To everything there is a season, and a time to every purpose under the heaven: A time to weep, and a time to laugh; a time to mourn, and a time to dance"

Just Walk Away

This is a tough one.

Walk away … Learn to walk away from toxicity.
Toxic environment. Toxic people. Toxic situations.

There is not much to say here if you don't want toxicity in
your space.

Stop entertaining it, take a deep breath, pat yourself on the shoulder and keep walking.
You will survive.
It gets better.

Life is just marvelous without toxicity.

Proverbs 22: 24-25 (KJV)

"Make no friendship with an angry man, and with a
furious man thou shalt not go:
Lest thou learn his ways, and get a snare to thy soul"

Evil Company Corrupts

Connect with buoyant people and laugh. Laugh heartily.

This is central to successful, happy, and joyful living (happy and joyful are two different things). Connecting with like-minded people is strength and fundamental to fostering friends and relationships. It gives a sense of belonging, dependability, and accountability. Optimistic people create environments for excelling in different ways.

Everyone wants to belong and be a part of something outside

of themselves. So, make it an auspicious one with much laughter. This would be good medicine for your soul.

1 Corinthians 15: 33 (NKJV)

"Do not be deceived: Evil company corrupts good habits"

Proverbs 17: 22 (KJV)

"A merry heart doeth good like a medicine: but a broken spirit drieth the bones"

It's More Blessed to Give

Consistency is paramount with this point. There is always someone less fortunate than you; give a helping hand. You were never meant to be a selfish being to gather all the spoils for yourself. There is an environmental law that's embedded in the principle of giving with a willing heart; the more you give, the more you will receive. The returns from this law are such that you will not be the only beneficiary, but it will also pass to your children and loved ones.

Some communities call this a blessing.

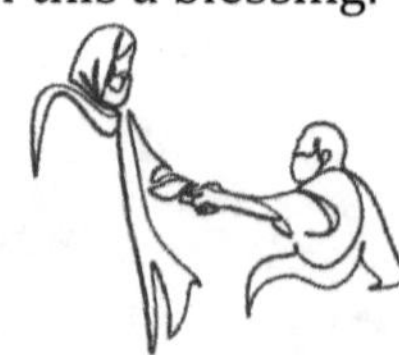

The act of giving will multiply the facets of your life's

mission. It is better to give than to receive because receiving is limited. You can utilize so much and no more. You can wear one pair of shoes at a time, but millions of people have no shoes to wear.

Isaiah 58: 10-11 (NKJV)

"If you extend your soul to the hungry and satisfy the
afflicted, then your light shall dawn in the darkness,
and your darkness shall be as the noonday. The Lord
will guide you continually, and satisfy your soul in drought,
and strengthen your bones; You shall be like a watered
garden,
and like a spring of water, whose waters do not fail"

Acts 20: 35 (KJV)

"I have shewed you all things, how that so laboring ye ought
to support the weak, and to remember the words of the Lord
Jesus, how he said, It is more blessed to give than to receive"

Epitome of Joy

Cultivate a spirit of thankfulness/gratefulness for the little things and the not-so-little things.

Who would have thought that thankfulness causes a physiological change in the body?

Having a thankful/grateful heart reduces anxiety and keeps you calm. This activates the parasympathetic nervous system, which helps with digestion and lowers blood pressure, heart rate, and breathing.

That's a mouthful to say that this nervous system helps you relax after a stressful episode.

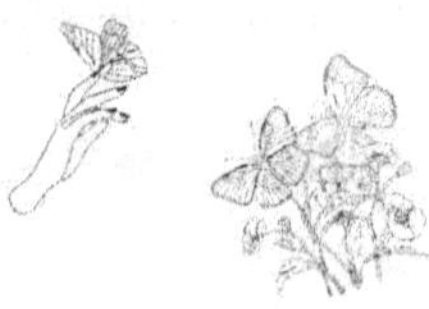

A heart of thankfulness/gratefulness is the epitome of joy.

We get caught up looking for happiness instead of joy.
Happiness is temporary.

1 Thessalonians 5: 16 &18 (KJV)

"Rejoice always. In everything give thanks: for
this is the will of God..."
(For you to live in joy)

Psalm 107: 21 (NKJV)

"Oh, that *men* would give thanks to the Lord *for*
His goodness, And *for* His wonderful works
to the children of men!"

Be Genuine

Celebrate every milestone, achievement and progress made towards a goal. Celebrate, genuinely, the people around you. Before you know it, you will have many great memories and an inclusive environment wherever you go. A life filled with great memories that were shared with others is a life worth living.

This type of achievement is Progress vs. Perfection.

Progress is a pragmatic mindset that involves making adjustments and improvements, learning from mistakes, and adapting to challenges. It is attainable, while perfection is not.

Zechariah 4: 10 (NLT)

"Do not despise these small beginnings, for the Lord rejoices to see the work begin…"

Romans 12: 15 (NKJV)

"Rejoice with those who rejoice…"

The Peace that Hums

At the end of each day, recount every occurrence with a smile because you made it through. Give Jehovah praise and glory for each occurrence. Acknowledging your Creator places you in a position of humility, which in and of itself is another level of joy.

There is a sweet peace that hums in the soul of men when there's a connection between the Creator and the created.

Jehovah cares about all your sorrows, joys and all that annoys. So, the conversation between you two should not be left to chance or be ignored. He has already chosen you to be His son/daughter, and it's now up to you to remain in that relationship.

Isaiah 41: 9 & 10 (KJV)

"...I have chosen thee, and not cast thee away.
Fear thou not; for I am with thee: be not dismayed; for I am
thy God: I will strengthen thee; yea, I will help thee;
Yea, I will uphold thee with the right hand
of my righteousness"

1 Peter 2: 9 (KJV)

"But ye are a chosen generation, a royal priesthood, a holy
nation, a peculiar people; that ye should shew forth the
praises of him who hath called you out of darkness into his
marvelous light;"

Within the Arms of Love

Don't forget to tell yourself those magical words, "I Love You". Lip service of these words will do you no good; say what you mean, mean what you say, and also believe what you say. Remember, love is an action word.

Pour into your love tank so that it may be filled and have an overflow that you will not run dry when you give from this vessel. You cannot give what you don't have.

Only those who love themselves can truly give love.

Within the arms of love, you will find the undercurrent of

another measure of strength, peace, confidence, and self-acceptance. However, love is gentle and pure on the outskirts but knows when to place boundaries to preserve itself.

2 Corinthians 8: 8 & 12 (NKJV)

"I speak not by commandment, but I am testing the sincerity of your love by the diligence of others. For if there is first a willing mind, *it is* accepted according to what one has, *and* not according to what he does not have"

1 Corinthians 13: 4-6 (NKJV)

"Love suffers long *and* is kind; love does not envy; love does not parade itself, is not puffed up; does not behave rudely, does not seek its own, is not provoked, thinks no evil; does not rejoice in iniquity, but rejoices in the truth"

NOTE TO SELF

Because my Abba Father has blessed me, I am enough,
and I promise to love me a little more.

I WILL KEEP THIS PROMISE!

The ways to unconditional love for myself and others are in
my hands, and I will be a force to be reckoned with when I
implement these attributes.
I am incredible!

Epilogue

The steps to loving yourself a little more are bold and will take much effort.

In life, I have learnt that people will do what's on their priority list and accomplish the tasks more easily when they are not complaining. Where on your priority list does loving yourself fall?

Broken promises tend to destroy confidence and trust and build walls of resistance to prevent future hurt. It would be a prudent thing not to break any promises you make to yourself.

Build the willpower and take the plunge to become a healthier and more loving version of yourself. You will not be able to contain your genuine sparks of love.

The best part of love is sharing it. And what better way to share such complex yet simple phenomena than from a place of genuineness?

Hurt people, hurt people.
What do you think of the opposite?
Loving people, love people.

Matthew 22: 36-39 (KJV)

"Master, which is the great commandment in the law?
Thou shalt love the Lord thy God with all
thy heart, and with all thy soul, and with all thy mind.
This is the first and great commandment.
And the second is like unto it, thou shalt love
thy neighbor as thyself"

About N. Nickola Freeman

An imagery poet, philanthropist, and nurse. She attended Northern Caribbean University, Jamaica, and graduated with honors in Nursing. While in school, she enjoyed working as an editor for some of her fellow schoolmates' term papers and writing speeches for oral presentations. She worked at her alma mater during her career, where she was first exposed to writing articles about health for the university's newspaper.

During her formative years, Nickola was constantly told that she could not read and was termed 'slow'. In her later years, she found out that she was a neurodivergent when she was diagnosed as being Dyslexic. The shackles of these labels were shattered when she embraced this trait as being a part of her and thus made the bold move to become an author. She has always sought to pour love and motivation into people; it's one of the most fulfilling moments for her to see people grow and blossom from her small seeds of constructive encouragement.

Nickola has published her first book, Apple Juice Martini, and is working on her next book, On the Pavement - the Giant, the Snail and the Ant.

Between nursing duties and writing, she develops her brand, Kola Love, using natural products for skin care and weight loss.
If you want to know more about Nickola and her brand, please connect with her at
https://www.instagram.com/pure_kolalove